BODYWORKS

skin and hair

Katherine Goode

BLACKBIRCH PRESS, INC.

WOODBRIDGE, CONNECTICUT

Published by Blackbirch Press, Inc.
260 Amity Road
Woodbridge, CT 06525

e-mail: staff@blackbirch.com
web site: www.blackbirch.com

Printed in Hong Kong

First published 1999 by
MACMILLAN EDUCATION AUSTRALIA PTY LTD
627 Chapel Street, South Yarra 3141

10 9 8 7 6 5 4 3 2 1

Photo Credits:
Cover photo: ©Dick Smolinski
Page 1: Graham Meadows Photography; pages 5, 27, 28: A.N.T.; page 18: AUSCAPE/©Dr. Zara; page 26: Coo-ee Picture Library; pages 7, 8, 9, 10, 13, 25: Great Southern Stock; page 16: HORIZON Photos; page 20: The Photo Library/©David Scharf; pages 4, 11, 12, 14, 15, 19, 24: The Picture Source; page 29: ©PhotoDisc.

Library of Congress Cataloging-in-Publication Data
Goode, Katherine, 1949–
Skin and hair / by Katherine Goode.
     p.   cm. — (Bodyworks)
    Includes index.
    Summary: Describes the functions, characteristics, disorders, and care of skin and hair.
    ISBN 1-56711-497-0 (hardcover : alk. paper)
    1. Skin—Juvenile literature. 2. Hair—Juvenile literature. [1. Skin. 2. Hair.] I. Title.
RL86.G66
611'.77—dc21
                                  00-008280
                                       CIP

Contents

The skin

Your skin is the layer of
tissue that covers your
body. It protects your
muscles and other
tissues. Your skin can
feel when it is touched.
It can also sense
changes in temperature.

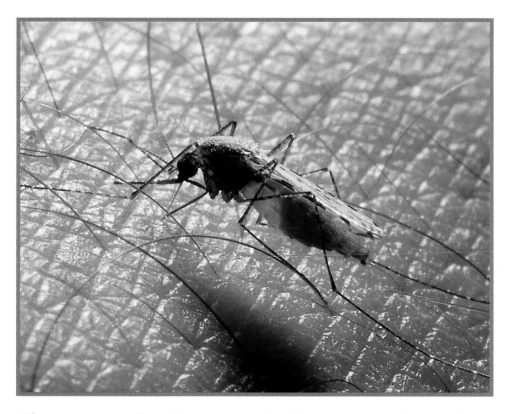

When a mosquito bites you, it pierces your skin and feeds on your blood.

Your skin helps keep fluids inside your body. It helps prevent germs and poisons from entering your body. It also protects the tissues under your skin from the sun's rays.

Parts of the skin

Your skin has 2 main layers. The outer layer is as thin as a piece of paper. It is called the epidermis. The inner layer contains sweat glands, blood vessels, oil glands, hair roots, and nerves. It is called the dermis.

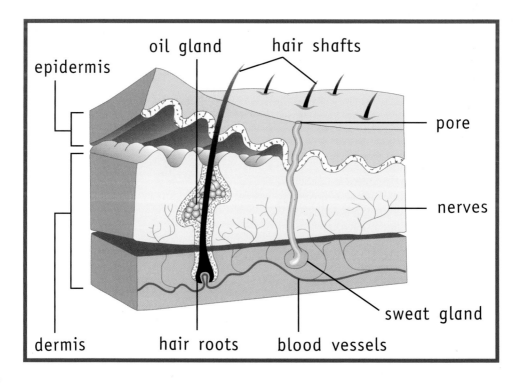

oil gland   hair shafts

epidermis

pore

nerves

sweat gland

dermis   hair roots   blood vessels

Sweat glands

When your body becomes too hot, you sweat. Your sweat glands release sweat through small holes in your skin called **pores**. Sweat cools your skin as it dries.

Blood vessels

When you are cold, the blood vessels near the surface of your skin become narrow. The blood flows more slowly and your body gives off less heat, so you stay warm for longer.

Thick clothes help to keep you warm in cold weather. They trap body heat close to your skin.

Oil glands

Your oil glands contain a fluid that makes your skin soft. Under the dermis, there is also fatty tissue, which stores fat. This fat helps to save body heat when the weather is cold. It also protects your body from injury.

When you bump into something, your fatty tissue usually protects your bones from breaking.

Your skin is elastic. It stretches as you grow. It is loose on most parts of your body. Your skin, however, is tightly attached to the tissues of your ears, the palms of your hands, and the soles of your feet.

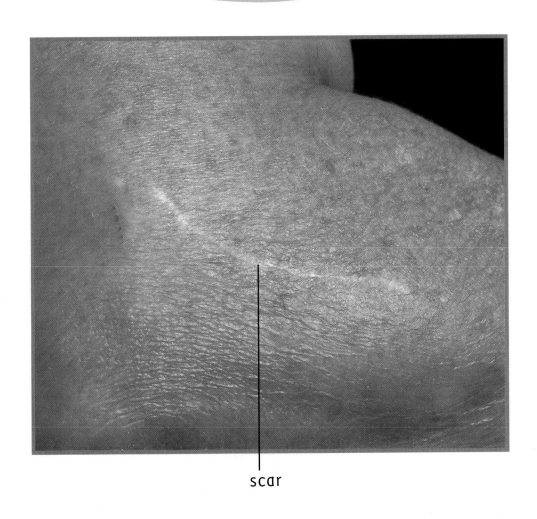

scar

Skin can repair itself. If your skin is cut, it will grow new cells over the injured area as it heals. If the cut is very deep, it will leave a scar.

Touch

Your skin contains nerves that can feel or sense touch. Your skin can sense the difference between tickling, patting, and hitting.

Your skin can also sense heat, cold, and pain.

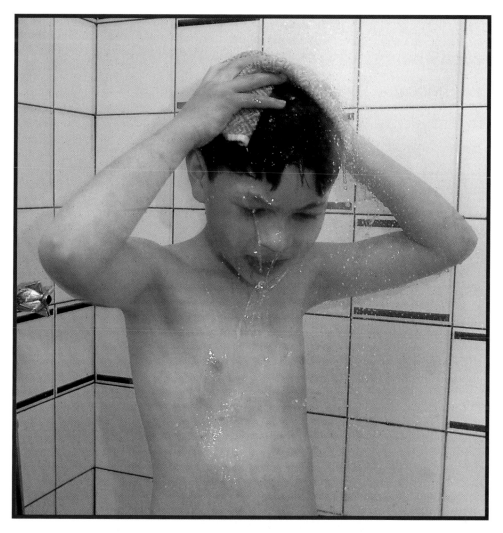

Nerves in your skin can feel the temperature of water.

Skin problems

Oil glands become more active when children reach their teens. When this happens, the skin can become more oily. The oil blocks the pores in the skin, which can cause **pimples**.

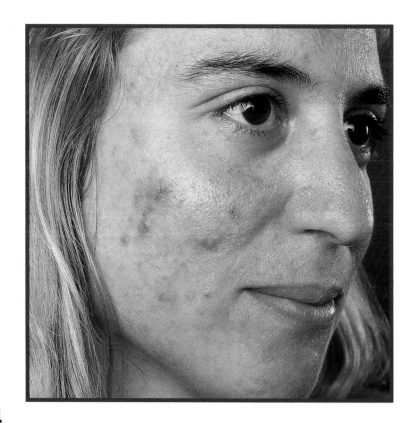

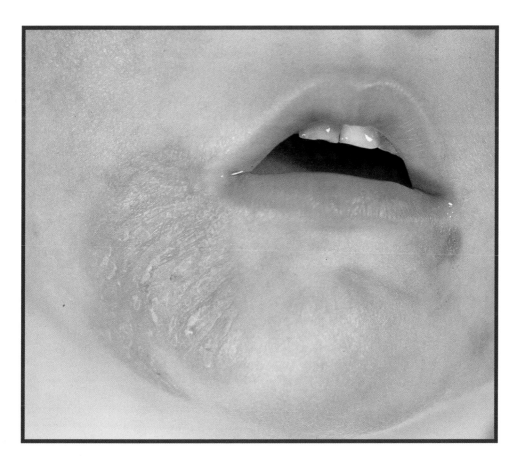

Eczema is a skin rash. Its causes are not known.

Measles, chicken pox, and some other illnesses can cause rashes on your skin. **Allergies** to food, animals, or plants can also cause rashes.

Skin pigment

Your skin contains a dark **pigment** called melanin. The color of your skin depends on how much pigment it has.

The sun may cause the color of your skin to
change. If the pigment in your skin is not
spread out evenly, then the sun may cause your
skin to freckle. If you stay out in the sun too
long, your skin may get sunburned.

Skin cancer

Sunburn destroys skin cells. It causes skin to flake and peel off. Damaged cells can sometimes develop into skin **cancer**, which is a serious problem. It means the skin cells are not growing back properly.

a skin cancer

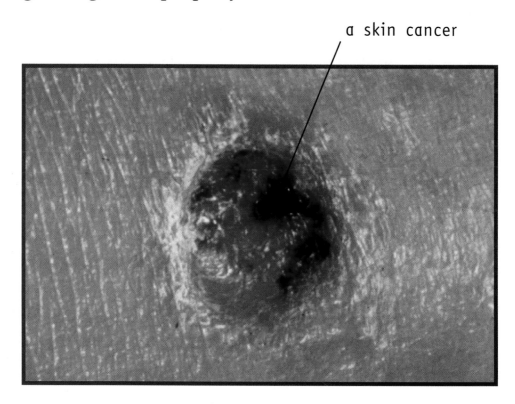

Skin care

You can protect your skin by wearing sunscreen and a hat. It is a good idea to stay out of the sun between 10 A.M. and 3 P.M., when the sun's rays are strongest.

The hair

Hair grows from roots in your skin. Thick hair grows on your head, and thinner hair grows on your body. Hair can be straight, wavy, or curly.

Close-up of hairs growing out of the head.

Like most mammals, humans have hair on their skin to help protect it. Eyelashes, eyebrows, nose hairs, and ear hairs screen out dust, sweat, and insects.

Parts of the hair

Your hair roots are in your skin. Each hair root begins in a soft, rounded hair bulb. The bulb is the only living part of your hair. It is where hair growth takes place.

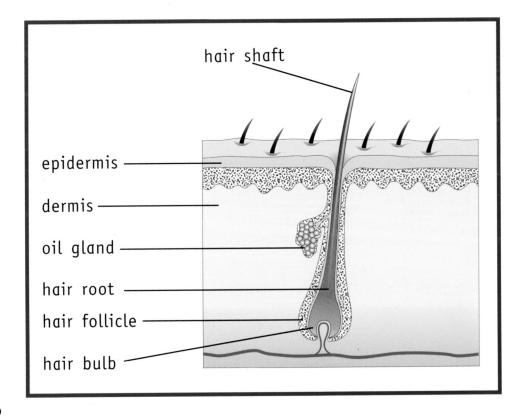

hair shaft

epidermis

dermis

oil gland

hair root

hair follicle

hair bulb

Each of your hair bulbs is lodged in a **follicle**. Your hair grows from the root and then pushes through the skin. It hardens and becomes a **shaft**. Oil glands attached to each hair soften it and make it shiny.

Hair color

Hair color depends on the amount of pigment in your hair. When people get older, the cells in their hair stop making pigment. Then their hair turns gray, or even white.

Hair loss

There are about 150,000 hairs on the human head. Sometimes people lose their hair and become bald. Baldness can be inherited, which is a trait that a person has at birth. It can also be caused by illness. More men than women become bald.

Animal hair

All mammals have hair on their bodies. Sheep have a woolly fleece. Pigs have stiff hair.

The tough, sharp hairs on an echidna's body are called quills.

Horns, hooves, and claws are made from the same material as hair.

Molting

Many animals shed their hair at certain times of the year. This is called molting. Some animals change color when they molt.

The arctic fox is brown in the summer.

In winter, the arctic fox's fur turns white.

At the end of summer, animals lose their lighter, summer coats. Then they grow thicker, warmer winter coats.

Hair care

Brushing your hair removes dirt and tangles. Dried oil from the oil glands can make your hair greasy. You can use shampoo to clean your hair.

Close-up of unwashed hair showing flakes of skin and dirt.

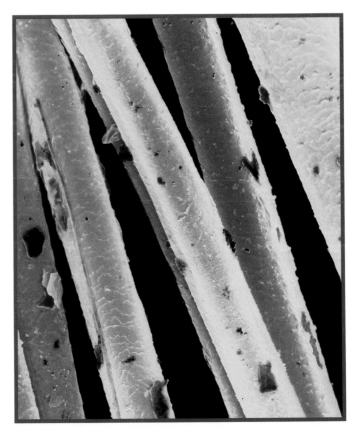

Glossary

allergy   a sensivity to certain foods, animals, or plants that causes sneezing or rashes

cancer   the harmful overgrowth of cells in the body, which causes illness and sometimes death

follicle   a tiny hole in the skin from which a single hair grows

pigment   the coloring materials found in skin, hair, and eyes

pimples   small, red swellings on the skin

pores   small openings in the skin

shaft   the part of the hair that grows out of the skin

tissue   the matter that living things are made of

Index